ALL THE TASTE

When I was invited to write a book entitled *"All the taste"*, I thought it was a great idea. Here was the chance to offer all visitors to our country a glimpse of our cuisine and to recreate it in their own homes! Despite the limited space available, I have endeavoured both to make sure that all Spain's communities or regions are represented in the book and to capture the spirit of our traditional cuisine and the Mediterranean diet.

Though briefly, we also mention the main Spanish DOC (Denomination of Origin) winemaking regions, followed by a short visit to the world of the tapa, so fashionable all over the world nowadays.

Then we come to a short section on soups and another on salads, traditional fare we could not possible ignore.

We then come to the recipes proper. These follow a logical order from starters to desserts to provide suggestions for the tastiest meals imaginable.

Finally, a practical alphabetical index enables readers to find their favourite recipes quickly and easily.

I very much hope that this book will bring back many happy memories, enabling lovers of Spain and its superb and varied cuisine to recreate some of its delights for family and friends.

Itos Vázquez

SPANISH WINES

There are at present 54 DOC (Designation of Origin) winemaking regions in Spain. Though all are more than worthy of mention, the map shows only the most important or representative of these, either due to their production or their recognised quality.

Spain produces and consumes enormous amounts of wine, offering superb value for money. Moreover, Spanish cuisine demands and finds a suitable wine for each different dish. We recommend that the dishes described in this book should be accompanied by a glass of good Spanish wine.

Although the conventions governing what type of wine is suitable for each different plate are now often ignored, many people still follow these criteria. What better, then, to accompany seafood or white fish than an Albariño white wine from the Rías Baixas in Galicia? Or a fine *reserva* Rioja to go with meat, or a *Gran Reserva* from the Ribera del Duero DOC to wash down an exquisite game dish?

Red wine from El Priorato, strong and full of body, is ideal for heavier dishes such as stew. For paella, perhaps the best wine we can recommend would be a rosé from Navarre or the Canary Islands, whilst blue fish, bonito or trout are best accompanied by a good white from Rueda. Game bird dishes such as pheasant go well with light reds from La Mancha or Valdepeñas. As an aperitif, try a sherry from Jerez or Cordoba, whilst with desserts there can be nothing better than a Pedro Ximénez or a muscatel from Jerez, Cordoba or Malaga.

Those preferring sparkling wine will find that "brut" cava accompanies the whole meal perfectly, whatever is on the menu. There is so much to choose from, and it is all well worth trying. One final tip: whatever Spanish region you find yourself in, try its wines they will also be ideal to accompany the local cuisine.

Finally, athough it is not a wine, we cannot fail to mention cider, the most famed drink in Asturias. Cider is made from apple juice, which is left to ferment for six months in wooden barrels. Expert barmen hold the bottle high up to pour it out into the glass in an impressive ceremony, after which it must be quaffed quickly before it goes flat.

Map of Spain's principal Denomination of Origin (DOC) wine regions. The most popular type of wine in each region is mentioned in brackets for each region.

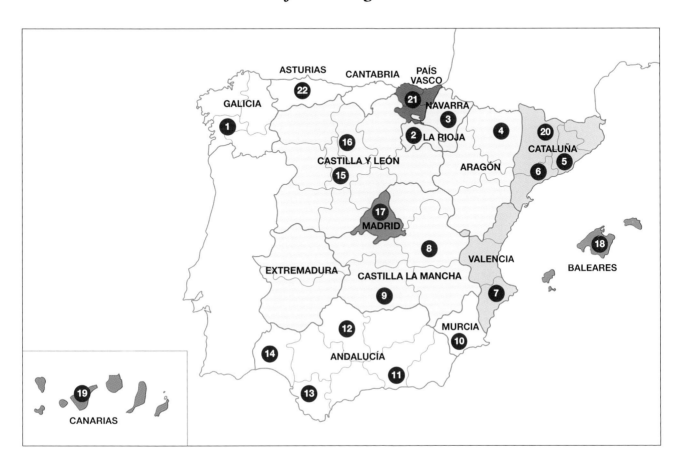

1. Rías Baixas (white) *Galicia*
2. La Rioja (red) *La Rioja*
3. Navarra (red and rosé) *Navarre*
4. Somontano (white and red) *Aragon*
5. Penedés (white and red) *Catalonia*
6. Priorato (red) *Catalonia*
7. Utiel-Requena (white and red) *Valencia*
8. La Mancha (red) *Castilla-La Mancha*
9. Valdepeñas (red) *Castilla-La Mancha*
10. Jumilla (red) *Murcia*
11. Málaga (Dulces) *Andalusia*
12. Moriles-Montilla (Fino, Amontillado, Oloroso and sweet sherry) *Andalusia*
13. Jerez-Xerés-Sherry y Manzanilla de Sanlúcar (Fino, Amontillado, Oloroso and sweet sherry) *Andalusia*
14. Condado de Huelva (white) *Andalusia*
15. Rueda (white) *Castilla y León*
16. Ribera del Duero (red) *Castilla y León*
17. Vinos de Madrid (white and red) *Madrid*
18. Binissalem (red) *Balearic Islands*
19. Tacoronte-Acentejo (red and rosé) *Canary Islands*
20. Cava (sparkling white) *Catalonia and others*
21. Txacolí (white) *Basque country*
22. Cider *Asturias*

TAPAS

Tapas, snacks often eaten whilst standing at the bar, is a culinary phenomenon fast becoming fashionable all over the world. Their origin is not known for certain, but would appear to go back to 18th-century Andalusia in the form of a slice of cold meat said to have been placed over wine glasses with the rather dubious purpose of keeping the many flies from falling into the precius liquid. Needless to say, this tasty morsel always ended up in the drinker's stomach, and the custom gradually evolved until small portions of tasty food, generally local products, were provided with drinks. These first tapas ("lids") were usually simple but tasty cold meats, particularly Iberian products. We shall present here just a small selection of Spanish tapas, for an exhaustive list would require a whole book devoted to these delightful titbits alone.

Chorizo a la Sidra (Salami in Cider)

Ingredients for 4 people

250 g chorizo (salami)

1/2 litre cider

Cut the salami into slices of 3 cm approximately. Place in a pan and cover in cider. Simmer for around 10 minutes, then serve.

Pinchitos de Riñones (Savoury Kidneys)

Ingredients for 4 people

6 lamb kidneys

12 mushrooms

12 cherry tomatoes

3 tablespoonfuls olive oil

ground black pepper

salt

Wash the kidneys well and cut them in half. Then skewer the kidneys onto cocktail sticks with washed mushrooms and tomatoes. Season and fry in hot oil. Serve while hot.

Boqueroncitos con Picadillo
(Savoury Anchovies)

Wash the red pepper and the tomatoes, peel the onion, and place the vegetables on the oven tray. Sprinkle with oil and roast. Once cooked, peel the red pepper and the tomatoes, chop and season with oil, vinegar and salt, mixing well. Put aside, then, wash the anchovies, drain well, lightly season, flour and fry in abundant hot oil. Dry on kitchen roll and serve while hot with the vegetable *picadillo*.

Ingredients for 4 people

500 g fresh anchovies
1 red pepper
1 medium-sized onion
2 ripe tomatoes
2 tablespoonfuls virgin olive oil
1 spoonful sherry vinegar
flour
olive oil for frying
salt

Soldaditos de Pavía (Fried Cod Sticks)

Ingredients for 4 people

400 g salt cod
4 spoonfuls of lemon juice
1 egg
flour
olive oil for frying

Soak the salt cod in water for 24 hours to remove the salt, changing the water three times. Dry, remove skin and bones and cut into small pieces or sticks. Place in a bowl, sprinkle with lemon juice and leave for 30 minutes. Then dry fish in kitchen roll, sprinkle with flour, dip in beaten egg and fry in plenty of hot olive oil. Dry on kitchen roll and serve hot.

Patatas Bravas (Potatoes in Spicy Sauce)

Ingredients for 4 people

500 g potatoes
1 cup of fried tomato
1/2 spoonful of vinegar
1 teaspoonful of tabasco sauce
olive oil for frying
salt

Wash the potatoes well and boil them in lightly salted water. Peel and cut into regular pieces. Heat oil in a deep pan and lightly fry potatoes and drain.
Meanwhile, mix the tomato with the vinegar and the tabasco. Place potatoes in a bowl and cover with the sauce. Serve hot or cold.

Salpicón de Mariscos (Seafood Cocktail)

Ingredients for 6 people

400 g octopus
250 g crabsticks
250 g cooked prawns
100 g cooked mussels
50 g black olives
1 spring onion
1 red pepper
1 green pepper
7 tablespoonfuls virgin olive oil
1 spoonful sherry vinegar
salt

Wash the octopus and beat it a little to make it more tender. Bring a large pan of salted water to the boil, put the octopus in and cook for 40 minutes or until tender. Slice and put aside.
Slice up the crabsticks. Wash and slice peppers. Peel and chop spring onion. Place octopus, mussels, prawns, crabsticks, olives, pepper and spring onion into a serving bowl. Add oil, vinegar and salt, and serve.

Champiñones con Jamón (Mushrooms With Ham)

Cut the stems off the mushrooms, leaving only the heads. Wash and dry in a clean cloth. Sprinkle with lemon to stop them going black and put aside.

In a large frying pan, heat oil and place the mushrooms in it face down, lightly frying for 5 minutes. Meanwhile, finely chop the ham and parsley. After 5 minutes, turn the mushrooms over, add ham and parsley, and season. Cover the pan and fry until golden and the ham has lost part of its fat. Serve hot.

Ingredients for 4 people

400 g mushrooms	parsley	3 tablespoonfuls olive oil	salt
100 g cured ham	1/2 lemon	ground pepper	

Tortilla Española (Spanish Omelette)

Peel the potatoes, wash them and cut into thin slices. Peel and chop the onion very fine. Heat plenty of oil in a pan and fry the potatoes and the onion on a low heat until they begin to become soft and golden. Remove potatoes with a turner and drain well.
Beat the eggs in a bowl, added the potatoes and the onion, season and mix well. Heat 2 spoonfuls of oil in the pan and, when hot, pour in mixture. Once cooked on one side, turn using a plate or lid and cook on other side. Serve freshly made or cold.

Ingredients for 4 people

6 eggs
600 g potatoes
1 large onion
1/2 cup olive oil
salt

SALADS

Healthy and refreshing, salads are an important and popular ingredient in the Mediterranean diet, both helping to break down fat in the body and providing gastronomic delight. Salads can be served either as a starter or to accompany a main dish. Sometimes, in Valencia, for example, it is even eaten after the main course, the paella. Salads become particularly popular all over Spain in the summer months, appealing much more to the palate than heavier dishes during the hot season.

Esqueixada (Salt Cod Salad)

Soak the cod in water for 24 hours to remove the salt, changing the water three times. Drain and dry well, remove skin and bones and cut into small pieces. Wash the tomatoes, grate and place in a colander to dry. Mix this purée with the cod, add the peppers, cut into strips (they can be grilled previously), the olives, the chopped garlic, salt, oil and vinegar. Mix gently and serve.

Ingredients for 4 people

250 g salt cod

500 g ripe tomatoes

2 green peppers

2 cloves of garlic

50 g de black olives

4 tablespoonfuls virgin olive oil

1 spoonful wine vinegar

salt

Ensalada Valenciana (Valencian Salad)

Ingredients for 4 people

1 small lettuce

2 tomatoes

200 g tuna fish in oil

2 eggs

1 small onion

50 g black olives

6 tablespoonfuls virgin olive oil

2 spoonfuls wine vinegar

salt

Separate the lettuce leaves, wash, drain well and chop fine, then place in salad bowl. Wash and chop the large, red tomatoes. Boil the eggs in salted water for 10-12 minutes according to size. Cool in cold water and peel. Chop up the tuna and the eggs and place with lettuce, add olives and onion, sliced into rings.

Make a vinaigrette sauce by mixing the oil, the vinegar and the salt. Season the salad and serve.

Ensaladilla Rusa (Potato Salad)

Ingredients for 4 people

800 g potatoes

2 carrots

1/2 cup peas

2 eggs

3 sweet peppers

100 g bonito in oil

2 cups mayonnaise sauce

1 lettuce heart

salt

Wash the potatoes and boil them in salted water until tender. Scrape the carrots, wash and place with peas in another saucepan, cover with water and boil for around 15 minutes. Boil the eggs for 10-12 minutes and leave to cool. Peel and dice the potatoes. Drain the peas and the carrots; chop the carrots and place vegetables in a salad bowl. Add one of the eggs, finely chopped, the bonito and half the mayonnaise. Mix, ensuring that the potatoes do not break up too much. Place the potato salad in a serving bowl and cover with the rest of the mayonnaise. Decorate with the other egg and the peppers, both sliced, and lettuce leaves.

Escalivada (Grilled Vegetable Salad)

Wash the aubergines, the peppers and the spring onions; sprinkle with oil and place on an oven tray. Preheat the oven and roast at medium temperature for 35-40 minutes.

Once the vegetables are cooked, peel the peppers, remove the seeds and cut into strips. Cut the aubergines into thick strips and the spring onions in half, lengthways. Place the vegetables in a bowl, season, sprinkle with crushed garlic and a dash of virgin olive oil.

Ingredients for 4 people

4 small aubergines

4 red peppers

1 bunch of spring onions

2 cloves of garlic

virgin olive oil

salt

SOUPS

The perfect start to a good meal. Hot or cold, soup is ever-present on Spanish menus, comforting or refreshing according to the season. Some of our soups, such as gazpacho, have become famed all over the world, representing Spain in the annals of international cuisine.

Gazpacho

Ingredients for 4 people

1 kilo ripe tomatoes

1 clove of garlic

1 cucumber

1 and 1/2 fine green peppers

50 g breadcrumbs

6 tablespoonfuls virgin olive oil

3 spoonfuls sherry vinegar

salt

*P*lace the clove of garlic, 1/2 cucumber, peeled and diced, one green pepper, washed, stem and seeds removed, and the breadcrumbs (soaked in water and drained) into the blender bowl with the vinegar and salt. Blend to make a purée. Wash and chop all the tomatoes except one, place in bowl and mix well. Strain well and beat while slowly adding a trickle of oil. Pour into a large bowl.

If soup is too thick, add cold water. Cool in fridge and serve with garnishing made from the remaining tomato, the clean, seeded pepper and the cucumber, skinned, all finely diced, but not mixed.

Ajo Blanco *(Garlic and Almond Soup with Grapes)*

Ingredients for 4 people

150 g raw almonds

2 cloves of garlic

200 g breadcrumbs

1 egg

1/2 cup virgin olive oil

2 spoonfuls sherry vinegar

grapes

salt

Place the almonds in cold water for 2 hours; if they are not peeled, before soaking them scald them for a few minutes in hot water and peel. Soak the breadcrumbs in cold water for about 5 minutes. Drain the breadcrumbs and place them in the blender bowl with the almonds, the egg, the peeled garlic, the vinegar and salt. Blend, then add oil little by little, beating all the time. Add cold water to obtain a light cream. Leave in the fridge for 2 or 3 hours. Serve with peeled, seeded grapes or, if you prefer, slices of apple or melon.

Sopa de Ajo *(Garlic Soup)*

Cut the bread into thin slices and put aside. Heat the oil in a pan and lightly fry the chopped garlic. Remove from heat, add paprika, season and stir with a wooden spoon.

Add the bread you have put by, and lightly fry. Add 6 cups of hot water, return pan to heat and cook gently for 15-20 minutes. Add salt to taste.

Pour into four individual bowls, break an egg into each, making sure the yolk does not break, and place under oven grill for 3 or 4 minutes until the eggs are cooked.

Ingredients for 4 people

200 g dry bread

4 cloves of garlic

5 tablespoonfuls olive oil

1 spoonful sweet paprika

50 g cured ham

4 eggs

salt

Sopa de Picadillo (Picadillo Soup)

Heat oil in pan and fry the chopped ham and the chicken livers, cleaned and sliced, until golden. Add the stock and boil gently for 30 minutes.

Add the rice, stir and boil gently for about 20 minutes until rice is cooked. Add seasoning to taste. Finally, pour the soup into a bowl, garnish with the sliced hard-boiled egg and serve hot.

Ingredients for 4 people

50 g cured ham	50 g rice	6 cups chicken stock	salt
6 chicken livers	1 hard-boiled egg	2 tablespoonfuls olive oil	

Migas Manchegas
(Fried Breadcrumbs from La Mancha)

This is a delicious country recipe for cold winter days, after a day's hunting, for instance.
Migas is a dish made practically all over Spain with slight variations, and which can be accompanied by grapes, sardines or practically any other garnishing.

Cut the bread into thin slices, place in a large bowl and sprinkle with salted water through a colander make it all equally moist. Cover with a cloth and leave to soak all night. Heat the oil in a pan and fry the chopped bacon and salami until it begins to turn golden brown. Remove, drain and put aside.

Peel the garlic and place whole cloves in the pan with the fat from the bacon and the salami, and fry until golden brown. Add the bread and stir until it is soaked in fat. Start to cut up the bread by beating it with the spoon or whisk.

When the bread is completely broken up into small pieces, return the salami and the bacon you put aside back to pan and continue beating. Add salt to taste and once the dish is ready, leave in the pan for a while without stirring to allow the bread to rest and the crust to form.

The source of the River Cuervo (Cuenca)

Ingredients for 6 people

500 g dry bread
200 g chorizo (salami)
150 g bacon
1 whole garlic
1/2 cup olive oil
salt

Marmitako
(Bonito or Tuna fish Soup)

A delicious dish from the north of Spain, a healthy, filling taste of the sea. Though originally from the Basque Country, marmitako is made all along the seaboard of Cantabria. In some places, salmon is used instead of tuna or bonito.

Ingredients for 4 people

500 g bonito (or tuna fish)	3 spoonfuls of dry white wine
3 "choricero" peppers	1 green pepper
1 large onion	2 cloves of garlic
800 g potatoes	4 tablespoonfuls olive oil
fish stock	salt
chopped parsley	
1/2 cup of fried tomato	

Pasai Donibane (Guipúzcoa)

Place the "choricero" peppers to soak for 20 minutes before cooking. Skin and bone the bonito or tuna, wash it and slice it up. Peel, wash and chop the potatoes. Wash the green pepper and cut it into strips. Peel and chop the onion and the garlic.

Heat the oil in a pan and sauté the onion and the garlic until transparent, then add the green pepper, the potatoes, the wine, the tomato, the flesh of the "choricero" peppers (scrape off with a knife) and stir everything together. Cover in stock and cook until the potatoes are tender. Season and add the bonito and the parsley, remove from heat and allow to rest for 2-3 minutes (the bonito will cook in the accumulated heat). Serve hot.

Cocido Madrileño

(Madridilenian Stew)

A classic dish from Spain's capital, mentioned in zarzuela and popular song, cocido is the most popular speciality amongst visitors to Madrid.

Soak the chickpeas for 12 hours in lukewarm salted water.

Put 2 litres of water into a large saucepan and add the stewing beef, the chicken, the eggs and the ham. Heat to boiling point and skim off foam. Season.

Madrid

Drain the chickpeas and place them in a net. Add them to the pot and cook for 2-3 hours. Chop the cabbage, cook it in a little stock from the stew and put aside, keeping it warm.

Midway through cooking (after an hour or an hour and a half) put in the carrots and the potatoes, peeled and whole, the salami and the black pudding. Complete cooking.

Once the chickpeas are tender, take out one litre of stock and cook the noodles in it (the amount depends on how thick the soup should be). Fry the garlic and add it to the drained cabbage. Serve the soup followed by the other ingredients.

Ingredients for 4 people

300 g chickpeas	100 g chorizo (salami)
300 g stewing beef	1 onion black pudding
1/4 kilo chicken	1 small cabbage
1 ham end	3 cloves of garlic
1 ham bone	3 carrots
1 knee bone	2 potatoes
1 beef bone	salt
150 g fresh bacon	
75 g medium noodles	

Potaje de Berros

(Watercress Broth)

This delicious broth comes from the Canary Islands, bringing nutrition and vitamins in a dish that perfectly complements the archipelago's marvellous climate.

Ingredients for 4 people

1 bunch of watercress (the leaves)

2 carrots

1 courgette

1 onion

150 g pumpkin

3 potatoes

300 g frozen sweetcorn

1/2 cup crushed tomatoes

2 cloves of garlic

1 litre stock

4 tablespoonfuls olive oil

ground pepper

salt

Tenerife

Peel, wash and chop the carrots, the pumpkin, the courgette and the potatoes. Heat the oil in a pan and lightly fry the onion and the finely-chopped garlic until the onion is transparent. Add the tomato, the carrots, the pumpkin, the courgette, the sweetcorn and the potatoes, the stock, salt and pepper, cover and cook gently for around 20 minutes.

Wash the watercress, place it in the pan, adding water if necessary, and cook for 10 minutes more or until it acquires the desired taste. Some of the soup can be passed through the blender to make it creamier if required.

Patatas a la Riojana
(Spicy Riojana Potatoes)

The famous French chef Paul Bocuse said of this dish that it was the most delicious he had ever tasted in his life. Indeed, washed down by a good Rioja wine, Patatas a la Riojana is a dish that comforts and raises the spirit.

Ingredients for 4 people

800 g potatoes
100 g bacon
100 g (salami) chorizo
2 sweet peppers
1 large onion
1/3 cup of white wine
1/2 spoonful sweet paprika
4 tablespoonfuls olive oil
salt

Logroño

Peel and wash the potatoes. Cut and gently open rather than slicing right through them with the knife.

Peel and chop the onion. Clean and slice the peppers. Heat the oil in an earthenware pan and lightly fry the potatoes, the onion and the peppers. Stir.

Meanwhile, cut the salami into slices, dice the bacon and add both to the pan with the paprika and salt, stir-fry and add the wine. Cover with water and simmer, stirring from time to time so that the sauce thickens without breaking up the potatoes.

Coliflor al Ajo Arriero
(Cauliflower in Garlic Sauce)

All "al ajo arriero" dishes come from Aragon, a land of hardy folk and robust but painstakingly-made wine. This is an easy dish to make, but the results are absolutely exquisite.

Ingredients for 4 people

1 small cauliflower

2 cloves of garlic

1 sprig of parsley

2 spoonfuls of breadcrumbs

5 tablespoonfuls olive oil

2 spoonfuls wine vinegar

1 spoonful sweet paprika

salt

Monasterio de Piedra (Monastery of Stone, Saragossa)

Remove the outer leaves and wash the cauliflower well, then place it whole in a pan and cover with cold water. Season and boil until cooked. Drain well and allow to cool a little. Then separate off the "flowerets", ensuring they do not break, and place in a serving bowl.

Heat the oil in a pan and fry the garlic, peeled and sliced, until golden. Remove from heat, add paprika, stir a little and add the bread and the vinegar, mixing well.

Pour the sauce over the cauliflower, sprinkle with chopped parsley and serve.

Arroz Negro

("Black Rice")

The cuisine of the Balearic Islands is both varied and tasty. "Arròs negre", as it is known on the islands, is an intense yet delicately flavoured example. On the coast or at home, reliving an unforgettable experience, this dish will delight friends and family alike.

Ingredients for 4 people

1 and 1/2 cups rice

500 g squid

1 medium-sized onion

300 g tomato

1/2 red pepper

1 green pepper

2 cloves of garlic

6 tablespoonfuls olive oil

4 and 1/2 cups fish stock

parsley

salt

Majorca

Wash the squid and slice it into rings, saving the ink. Heat the oil in an earthenware pan and fry the squid for 3-4 minutes.

Add the chopped onion and lightly fry until transparent. Add the peeled and crushed tomatoes and the chopped peppers. Lightly fry for 10-15 minutes on a low heat. Pour in 1 cup of the stock and add the parsley and the garlic and simmer for another 10 minutes.

Mix the ink into the remaining stock and add to the pan. When it begins to boil, add the rice. Simmer for 18-20 minutes, until the rice is cooked. Season to taste and serve hot.

Fabada Asturiana

(Asturian Bean Stew)

This is the most typical dish in the Asturias region, an exquisite dish, strong and richly-flavoured. Accompanied by a robust wine or a bottle of cider, Fabada Asturiana is a meal in itself.

Ingredients for 8 people

750 g white beans

200 g bacon

4 chorizos (salamis)

2 black puddings

200 g salt pork

1 end of ham

200 g shoulder of pork

saffron

salt

Mount Covadonga

Soak the beans in cold water overnight. Drain and place in a large pan, cover with cold water and heat. When it starts boiling, throw away the water and cover with cold water again. Add the bacon, the salamis, the salt pork, the end of ham and the shoulder of pork. Simmer for 2-3 hours.

Half-way through cooking, dilute the saffron in 4 spoonfuls of stock from the beans and add this mixture to the pot. Around 10-15 minutes before the end, add the black pudding, previously washed.

Before serving the stew, take out a few beans and crush them into a paste with a fork. Add this to the stock and stir until it thickens a little. Serve hot.

Paella

Paella is the name of the recipient in which this universal rice dish is prepared. Although originally from Valencia, paella is renowned as one of the most typical dishes in Spanish cuisine in general. A possible variant is paella made from fish and seafood only.

Ingredients for 6 people

600 g rice	2 green peppers	1 large squid
500 g mussels	1 red pepper	100 g processed peas
200 g prawns	1 and a 1/2 litres chicken stock	1/2 cup olive oil
300 g chicken	saffron	3 cloves of garlic
250 g pork chops	1/2 teaspoonful paprika	parsley
150 g green beans	200 g sweet pepper	salt

Wash the chicken and the chops; clean the mussels; peel the prawns, wash the squid and cut it into rings. Peel and chop the tomatoes, wash and cut the peppers into strips; clean and chop the beans. Heat a cup of water in a pan and place mussels in the boiling water to open them. Drain and put the liquid by. Simmer the prawn shells and heads in 3 cups water for 15 minutes; drain and put by.

Heat the oil in a *paella* or large, round shallow pan and fry the chicken and the chops; add the squid, the peppers, the tomato and the green beans, and lightly fry for a further 10 minutes; add 1 cup of the stock put by and cook gently. When the stock has begun to evaporate, add the rice and lightly fry for a few minutes, stirring with a wooden spoon until well mixed. Cover with warm stock or water, adding approximately two parts liquid to one part rice. Add the peas and chopped parsley, garlic, saffron, paprika and salt. Heat strongly for 10 minutes, then reduce heat, place mussels, prawns and sweet pepper, cut into strips, on the top of the rice and simmer for 8-10 minutes. Remove from heat, allow to rest for 3-4 minutes, then serve.

Arroz con Costra
(Savoury Rice with a Crusty Topping)

Murcia is a region rich in vegetables and pork. Arroz con Costra, a typical inland dish in this autonomous community, really begs to be accompanied by a strong Murcian wine from Jumilla or Yecla, the perfect complement for this rice dish made from local produce.

Ingredients for 4 people

350 g rice	2 cloves of garlic
50 g spicy salami	3 eggs
50 g chorizo (salami)	1 spoonful grated cheese
50 g cured ham	5 tablespoonfuls olive oil
30 g longaniza pork sausage	6 strands of saffron
50 g pickled artichokes	1 spoonful of chopped parsley
1 sweet pepper	salt

The "Alcantarilla Wheel" (Murcia)

Heat the oil in an earthenware pan and peel and fry the whole garlic cloves until golden. Remove garlic and crush in mortar with the parsley and the strands of saffron.

Peel the skin off the salami and the *longaniza* and chop the salami, the *longaniza*, the ham and the pepper. Place in pan with the oil, stir, add the artichokes, and lightly fry for a few minutes. Add two parts water or stock for one part rice and place in pan along with the finely chopped herbs. When it boils, add the rice, stir, season and simmer for 10 minutes.

Whisk the eggs in a bowl, add the grated cheese, mix and pour onto the rice, place in a hot oven and continue cooking for a further 8-10 minutes or until the topping becomes golden. Leave to rest for a couple of minutes, then serve.

Fideuá

An original alternative to paella, just as delicious. Complemented to perfection by a good rosé, particularly if from Valencia.

Ingredients for 4 people

300 g thick noodles
300 g prawns
250 g cuttlefish, sliced into rings
4 Norway lobsters
1 slice of chilli pepper
200 g fresh crushed tomato
2 cloves of garlic
4 tablespoonfuls olive oil
the juice of 1/2 lemon
parsley
salt

La Albufera (Valencia)

Peel the prawns and cook the shells and heads in salt water for 10 minutes; drain and put by. Heat the oil in a *paella* and lightly fry the Norway lobsters on either side. Remove and put by. Add the cuttlefish rings and lightly fry for a few minutes; add the tomato and the chilli pepper and fry for about 10 minutes.

Add 2 cups of the stock put by (add more if necessary), along with the chopped garlic, parsley and the lemon juice. Mix well and begin to simmer, adding the noodles, spreading them evenly around the pan. Salt to taste and simmer for about 10 minutes. Add the prawns, place the Norway lobsters on top and continue simmering until the noodles are cooked. Leave to rest for a few minutes, then serve.

Caldereta de Langosta
(Lobster Casserole)

The King of Spain visits Cala Fornells on the island of Majorca every year to enjoy this peerless dish. With "sobrasada" red sausage on toast as a starter, caldereta provides the main course in an incomparable yet easy-to-prepare Majorcan meal.

Ingredients for 6 people

2 lobsters, each weighing 1 kilo
2 large onions
3 tomatoes
1 litre of fish stock
5 tablespoonfuls olive oil
2 cloves of garlic
1 laurel leaf
1 spoonful of chopped parsley
6 slices of farmhouse bread
ground black pepper
salt

Minorca

Boil the lobsters en 1.5 litres of salted water for 10 minutes. Take out and put by. Heat the oil in an earthenware pan and lightly fry the onions, the garlic and the parsley, all finely chopped, for 10 minutes. Add the chopped tomatoes and lightly fry for 15 or 20 minutes or until a thick sauce is obtained. Blend and return to the frying pan.

Add the lobsters, the laurel, the fish stock and the lobster stock, add salt and pepper and simmer for 10-15 minutes on a low heat.

To serve, place thin slices of bread on plates and pour the casserole over it, with the lobsters cut into small pieces.

Pulpo a Feira
(Galician-Style Octopus)

Following the instructions carefully and ensuring that the octopus is done to a turn will assure you all the taste of one of Galicia's most emblematic dishes. It is essential, also, to use good paprika and extra virgin olive oil.

Ingredients for 6 people

2 kilos octopus
4 laurel leaves
1 spoonful sweet paprika
1 spoonful hot paprika
1 cup extra virgin olive oil
kitchen salt

Combarro (Pontevedra)

Wash the octopus and dry using kitchen roll. Freeze so that it softens without beating. Leave to defrost. Heat water in a pan, adding laurel. Submerge the octopus in the water several times, tentacles down, finally leaving it in the water once boiling. Simmer for 30 or 40 minutes, testing with a fork from time to time until the octopus is tender. Remove from heat, take out from water and leave to rest 15 minutes so that the skin comes off.

Cut into slices, not too thick. Place these on one or more wooden plates, add kitchen salt and sweet and hot paprika, and sprinkle with oil. Serve with boiled potatoes or other accompaniment.

Dorada a la Sal

(Gilthead Seabream in Salt)

Known locally as dorada, gilthead seabream is found all along the Andalusian coastline, as well as in many other regions and countries. Cooked in salt, it conserves all its delicate flavour and makes a truly spectacular and delicious main course.

Ingredients for 4 people

1 gilthead seabream (1.5 kilos)
2 kilos of kitchen salt
mayonnaise or vinaigrette sauce

The Alhambra Palace (Granada)

Leaving the fish whole, with scales and innards, wash well and allow to dry. Use half the salt to cover the bottom of an oven dish and place the fish over it. Cover with the rest of the salt, pressing it with the hands to make a firm coating. Heat the oven and bake the fish at medium temperature (180º C) for about 20-30 minutes, depending on the size of the fish.

Remove salt and serve with mayonnaise or vinaigrette sauce and boiled potatoes.

Salmón a la Sidra
(Samon in Cider)

In the early-19th century, Asturian coal-miners demanded not to be given salmon more than three times a week. Nowadays, this delicious fish sells at the highest prices if caught in the rivers of that Spanish region.

Ingredients for 4 people

800 g salmon
250 g mushrooms
1 cup cider
1 teaspoonful maize flour
ground white pepper
1 laurel leaf
salt

Gijón

Wash the salmon and remove scales. Wash the mushrooms thoroughly, changing the water several times, drain and chop. Place the salmon in an oven dish, season and place the chopped mushrooms around and over it. Sprinkle with chopped laurel leaf. Sprinkle with cider and cover with silver paper.

Bake in a hot oven at medium temperature for about 12 minutes, according to the size of the fish. Open the silver paper and remove some stock from dish, putting it into a small saucepan and mixing with maize flour, previously dissolved in a spoonful of water. Serve the salmon immediately with the mushrooms and the sauce.

Besugo a la Espalda
(Bream "A la Espalda")

Besugo -bream- is one of the most exquisite fish to be found on the Spanish coast. Though eaten practically all year round, it has long been a classic on the Christmas Eve dinner menu and is particularly appreciated in the Basque Country.

Ingredients for 4 people

1 seabream (weighing approx. 1.25 kilos)
1/2 cup olive oil
4 cloves of garlic
Wine vinegar
chilli pepper (optional)
salt

Bilbao

Wash the fish, remove backbone and open out. Place in an oven dish, lightly season and bake in preheated oven at medium temperature for 15-20 minutes approximately, according to the size of the fish.

Heat oil in a pan and golden fry the sliced garlic and chilli pepper; remove from the heat and add a dash of vinegar. Pour the mixture over the fish and serve immediately, accompanied by potatoes cooked "a lo pobre".

Sardinas a la Marinera

(Sardines a la Marinera)

Sardines from Cantabria are famed for their excellence, grilled and eaten in bars and port restaurants. This rather more elaborate recipe brings out all the rich flavour of this humble but exquisite fish.

Ingredients for 4 people

800 g small sardines
1 kilo tomatoes
2 green peppers
1 large onion
2 cloves of garlic
6 tablespoonfuls olive oil
1 sprig of parsley
ground pepper
salt

Santander

Remove head and innards from sardines, scrape, wash and leave to drain.

Scald the tomatoes in boiling water for 2 minutes, leave to cool, peel and finely chop. Place tomatoes in a bowl with the onion, the chopped peppers, salt and half the oil.

Arrange a layer of vegetables at the bottom of an earthenware pan, cover with a layer of sardines, season and sprinkle with finely-chopped garlic and parsley. Continue adding layers, adding a final layer of sardines. Sprinkle with the remaining oil, cover with silver paper and place in a hot oven at low temperature for 1 hour approximately.

Bacalao al Pil-Pil

(Pil-Pil Cod)

Bacalao al pil-pil is another essential dish in Basque cuisine. As so often is the case, the recipe was discovered by chance. It is important to shake the pan gently but constantly for the sauce to thicken properly.

Ingredients for 4 people

800 g boneless salt cod, cut into pieces

1 cup virgin olive oil

6 cloves of garlic

chilli pepper

Mutriku (Guipúzcoa)

Place the cod in a bowl and cover in cold water. Leave for 48 hours, changing the water three times. Drain and bone carefully so as not to break the fish, and dry.

Heat the oil in an earthenware pan, fry the sliced garlic until golden with the chopped, seedless chilli pepper. Take out and put by.

Let the oil cool a little, then place the cod in the frying pan, skin down. Place on heat, lowering heat once the cod begins to warm up, ensuring that the oil does not boil. When the cod begins to break up, take off heat. Move the pan from side to side constantly for about 15 minutes, until the sauce thickens. Decorate with the garlic and the chilli pepper, and serve immediately.

Pollo al Chilindrón
(Chicken with Pepper and Tomatoes)

Dishes made "al chilindrón" require peppers, which combine very well with meat and poultry, particularly lamb and chicken, giving them extraordinary flavour. Such dishes are particularly popular in Aragon and La Rioja.

Ingredients for 4 people

1 chicken (1.25 kilos, approx.)
150 g cured ham
1 large onion
3 cloves of garlic
500 g crushed fresh tomato
1 red pepper
1 green pepper
4 tablespoonfuls olive oil
ground black pepper
salt

Saragossa

Wash and dry the chicken, quarter it and season. Heat the oil in a pan and lightly fry the peeled garlic, then take it out and throw it away. Lightly fry the chicken in the same pan. Add the ham and onion, both chopped. When the onion is transparent, add the peppers, washed and cut into slices, and the tomato. Season and fry gently for approximately 1 hour until the chicken is tender.

Serve in a bowl, adorning to taste, with strips of pepper on top.

Mar y Montaña
(Lobster and Chicken Casserole)

Though traditionally made with lobster, this recipe can also be made with prawns. "Mar y Montaña" is an exquisite Catalan dish that perfectly blends two opposing flavours.

Ingredients for 6 people

1 chicken (1.5 kilos, approximately)
2 lobster tails
1 large onion
500 g ripe tomatoes
4 spoonfuls oil
1/2 cup brandy
1 laurel leaf
oregano
ground black pepper
salt

Costa Brava

Wash the chicken, removing excess fat, and dry with kitchen roll. Cut into pieces and season. Heat the oil in a pan and lightly fry the chicken. Take out, drain and put by.

In the same oil as the chicken, lightly fry the chopped onion until it becomes transparent; add the peeled and crushed tomatoes, the oregano, the laurel, salt and pepper, and simmer for 12-15 minutes. Add the chicken pieces, sprinkle with the brandy, cover and continue cooking until the meat is tender. Add the peeled lobster tails and simmer for 1-2 minutes according to thickness. Serve the chicken with the lobster tails cut into slices.

Cochinillo Asado

(Roast Suckling Pig)

A classic from the cuisine of Segovia, roast suckling pig is said to be done to a turn when you can cut it using the side of a flat plate, and indeed some Segovian restaurants do just this. And what better accompaniment for this rich satisfying dish than a good Ribera de Duero DOC red wine!

Ingredients for 6 people

Half a suckling pig (2 and 1/2 kilos)
1 head of garlic
500 g potatoes
1 large onion
1/2 cup white wine
1/4 cup olive oil
100 g lard
ground pepper
salt

Segovia

Wash and dry the suckling pig. Singe off any hair on the ears, legs, etc, over an open flame and grease thoroughly with lard. Season. Place wooden spoons on the oven tray to make a grille (laurel cuttings can be used instead of spoons). Place the suckling pig with the skin up. Heat the oven to full power. Wet the suckling pig with salted water and roast it at medium temperature for 1 hour, until the skin is crisp and golden. Peel the potatoes and the onion and cut them into 1/2 cm thick slices. Take out the suckling pig from the oven, remove the spoons and arrange the onion and the potatoes at the bottom of the tray with the suckling pig on top. Sprinkle with wine and put it in the oven for about 50 minutes or until the meat is tender and well-cooked.

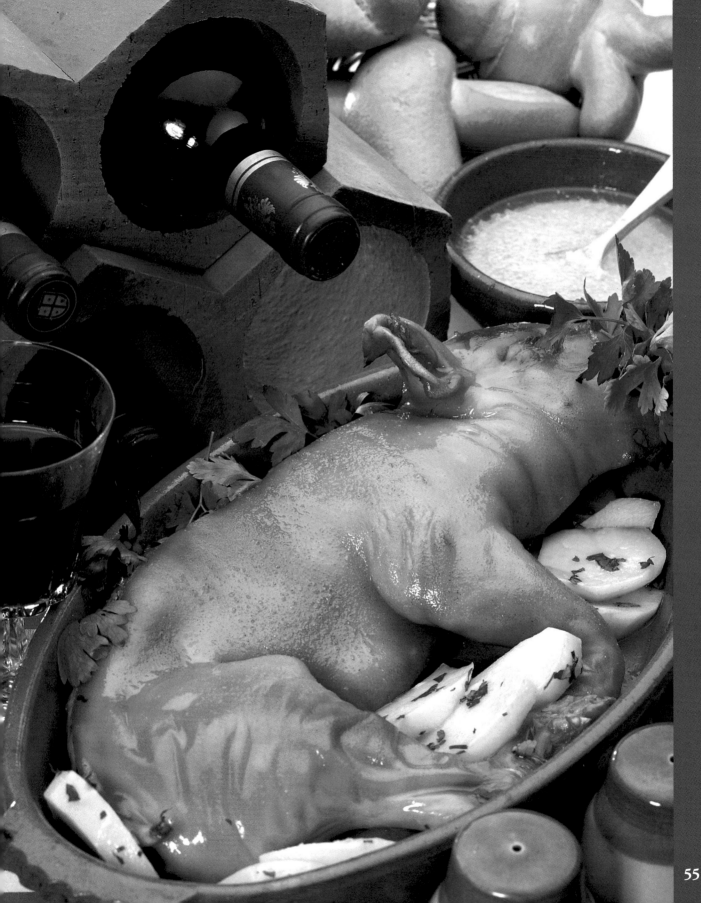

Caldereta de Cordero Extremeña

(Extremadura Lamb Casserole)

The cuisine of Extremadura is robust and strongly-flavoured. Fitting for a land of "conquistadores", who needed to feed up well in preparation for their long, often perilous voyages.

Ingredients for 4 people

1 kilo lamb, chopped

500 g potatoes

1 green pepper

1/2 red pepper

1 large onion

2 tomatoes

3 cloves of garlic

2 carrots

1/2 teaspoonful of cumin

6 corns of black pepper

1 laurel leaf

1/2 spoonful sweet paprika

6 tablespoonfuls olive oil

1/2 cup white wine

salt

Villanueva de la Vera (Cáceres)

Place the lamb in a pan with the laurel, cover with cold water and heat. When it starts boiling, skim off the froth and simmer for 1 hour.

Meanwhile, lightly fry in oil the chopped onion, 2 cloves of crushed garlic, the peppers, washed and sliced, the peeled and crushed tomatoes and the carrots, scraped and sliced. Simmer for 20 minutes.

Crush the rest of the garlic, salt, paprika, the corns of pepper and the cumin in a mortar. Add the lamb, the finely chopped herbs and the wine and simmer for 45 minutes or until the meat is tender. Finally, add the potatoes, peeled washed and chopped, and simmer for another 20 minutes. Season and serve hot immediately.

Morteruelo

This dish, ancient in origin, is famous particularly in the Castilian city of Cuenca. Though it can test the hardiest digestive system, taken in moderation, morteruelo is as delicious as the best paté money can buy.

Ingredients for 8 people

250 g chicken	5 walnuts
250 g hare	5 corns of black pepper
250 g pork liver	1 spoonful sweet paprika
200 g sirloin pork	2 cloves
3 cloves of garlic	1/2 teaspoonful of powdered cinnamon
1 and 1/2 cups breadcrumbs	1/2 teaspoonful of ground caraway seeds
2 cups stock	toasted bread
3 tablespoonfuls olive oil	salt

Cuenca

Wash and drain the meat. Peel and chop the garlic. Heat oil in a pan and lightly fry the garlic. Add the pieces of meat, frying until golden all over. Place in a saucepan, cover with water and simmer, with the lid on, for 45 minutes or until tender.

Take out the meat from this stock and drain well. Bone and chop meat with a sharp knife. Blend the liver until it becomes a cream.

Place the cooking stock in a pan and add the chopped meat, the liver purée and a ground mixture of the grated bread, the walnuts, peeled and chopped, the grated cloves, the peppercorns, the ground caraway seeds, the paprika and the cinnamon, previously diluted with a little stock. Simmer for 20 minutes, then serve with toast.

Pierna de Cordero al Horno

(Roast Leg of Lamb)

You can find lamb in practically every country in the world, but lamb from La Mancha is unmatched in its texture and flavour. So much so, that just a little lard and a little water can turn it into the most exquisite dish imaginable. Restaurants all over Castile prepare this dish for the delight of locals and visitors alike.

Ingredients for 8 people

1 leg of lamb (1.5 kilos, approximately)
2 spoonfuls of lard
1/2 cup brandy
400 g small potatoes
ground black pepper
salt

Chinchilla de Montearagón (Albacete)

Wash the lamb under the tap and dry it with kitchen roll. Season and grease with melted lard.

Place the leg of lamb in an earthenware pan and roast it in a hot oven at medium temperature for about 1 hour and a half. After approximately 45 minutes, when the surface is golden, sprinkle the meat with the brandy and add the potatoes, peeled and washed (add a little water if dry). Serve very hot.

Callos a la Madrileña

(Tripe Madrid Style)

This is the "other" Madrilenian dish par excellence. A traditional local dish, found in restaurants, tascas and tabernas, callos a la madrileña is similar to many dishes found in Latin America, where it was introduced by the 15th-century explorers. A powerful dish, this is best accompanied by a good Valdepeñas wine.

Ingredients for 6 people

1 kilo tripe	1 laurel leaf
1 veal trotter	chilli pepper
100 g cured ham	2 cloves of garlic
1 chorizo (salami)	3 sprigs of parsley
1 black pudding	4 tablespoonfuls olive oil
1 large onion	saffron
1 tomato	salt
1 spoonful of flour	

Madrid

Wash the tripe and the veal trotter well, place in a pan, cover with water and simmer until tender (approximately 2 hours).

Heat the oil in a pan and lightly fry the chopped onion. Add the peeled, chopped tomato, stir, add flour, simmer and add part of the stock from cooking the tripe.

Place the contents of the frying pan into the saucepan, along with the ham, the salami, the black pudding, the laurel and the chilli pepper, finely chopped garlic, salt, the parsley and the saffron; cover and simmer for another 1/2 hour (the stock should become thick).

Lacón con Grelos

(Shoulder of Pork with Turnip Tops)

Shoulder of pork is the front leg, whilst "grelos" -turnip tops-
typical of Galicia, can be replaced by silver beet, though the
flavour changes somewhat. A comforting, strong dish
for cold days.

Rías Baixas

Ingredients for 4 people

500 g fresh shoulder of pork
500 g turnip tops
300 g white beans
25 g grease
salt

Wash the turnip tops and cut them into small pieces. Wash the shoulder of pork and boil it in a pan with water on low heat for 2 hours or until the meat is tender.

Place the beans, soaked overnight, in a pan, cover with cold water and cook gently, adding cold water three times. When the beans are nearly done (after about 1 and a half to 2 hours), add the grease and continue cooking. When cooked, add the chopped turnip tops and the shoulder of pork, tender by now.

Season and continue cooking for about 10 minutes or until the turnip tops are done. Serve hot, with plenty of stock.

Chivo Estofado
(Kid Stew)

"Chivo estofado" is one of the most typical Canary Island recipes. Kid meat, full of flavour, is reminiscent to the palate of milder game dishes found on the Peninsula.

Ingredients for 4 people

800 g kid meat
1 large onion
1 green pepper
400 g crushed fresh tomatoes
3 cloves of garlic
4 tablespoonfuls olive oil
1 sprig of parsley
1/2 cup red wine
2 laurel leaves
chilli pepper
salt

Gran Canaria

Wash the meat, dry and cut into pieces. Peel and chop the onion and the garlic. Remove seeds from pepper and chop.

Heat the oil in a pan and fry the meat until golden all over. Add the garlic and the onion and lightly fry. Add the chilli pepper, the crushed tomato and the pepper. Stir, season and lightly fry for 10 minutes. Sprinkle with wine and add the herbs. Stir, add a little water or stock and simmer very gently until the meat is tender (approximately 1 hour).

Serving suggestion: accompanied by rice with saffron or any other garnishing.

Filloas
(Galician-Style Pancakes)

The best way to round off a meal in Galicia is with a plate of filloas and a glass of good orujo brandy. They are delicious. If only they weren't so fattening!

Ingredients for 8 people

300 g flour

3 eggs

50 g butter

4 cups milk

100 g sugar

4 egg yolks

the peel from 1/2 lemon

1 sprig of cinnamon

icing sugar

Galicia

To make the batter: mix 250 g flour with the eggs, the melted butter and 2 cups of milk, little by little, mixing well. Leave to rest for 1 hour.

To make the cream filling: heat the remaining milk with the lemon skin and the cinnamon. Whisk the egg yolks with 100 g sugar and the remaining flour, sieved. Add the milk little by little, whisking all the while and place on heat until the cream thickens. Allow to cool.

To make the pancakes: heat a non-stick frying pan and grease with butter. Pour in batter, spreading well. Once one side is golden, turn and lightly fry the other side. Use all the batter in this way. Fill the pancakes with the cream, roll, sprinkle with icing sugar and serve.

Leche Frita

(Fried Custard Squares)

The cuisine of Navarre superbly combines meat with garden produce. An ideal complement to round off such a meal is "leche frita", a cheap, easily made dessert originally made by convent nuns.

Ingredients for 4 people

1/2 litre milk
100 g flour
100 g sugar
3 eggs
1 sprig of cinnamon
the peel from 1 lemon
1 spoonful of butter
powdered cinnamon
olive oil for frying

Navarre

Mix 60 g flour, the sugar, 2 eggs and a little milk in a pan, stirring so that there are no lumps. Heat the remaining milk with the cinnamon and the lemon skin and pour onto the mixture. Heat, stirring to make sure it doesn't stick, until thick. Pour into a bowl, greased with butter (it should rise to about 2-3 cm in height). Leave to cool for a few hours in the fridge.

Cut into squares, dip in flour and whisked egg and fry in abundant hot oil. Drain on kitchen roll and sprinkle with sugar and cinnamon.

Tocino de Cielo

(Egg Yolk and Syrup Pudding)

Although the origins of this fantastic dessert ("Pork from Heaven") appear to go back to a monastery in northern Portugal, the recipe was perfected in the convents of Andalusia, near the wineries, where egg white was used to clear the wine and the unwanted yolks were given to the local nuns.

Ingredients for 8 people

12 egg yolks
450 g sugar
1 cup water

Make a caramel with 3 spoonfuls of sugar and 1 of water, and caramelise a large rectangular mould or several smaller ones. In a pan, make syrup from water and the remaining sugar. When the syrup is about to boil, take from heat and allow to cool a little.

Whisk the egg yolks in a bowl and add the syrup, stirring all the while, mixing well. Pour into the caramelised mould or moulds. Cover with silver paper and bake in the oven, in a double saucepan, for 30 minutes or until it sets. Leave to cool and take out from mould. Decorate with meringue or cream and serve.

Córdoba

Crema Catalana
(Catalan Custard Cream)

A dessert that is now made industrially, decreasing its quality. When homemade, this is one of Spanish cuisine's finest sweets.

Ingredients for 6 people

1 litre milk
6 egg yolks
300 g sugar
2 spoonfuls of maize flour
the peel from 1/2 lemon

Montserrat

*H*eat the milk with the lemon peel, taking off heat when it begins to boil. Meanwhile, whisk the egg yolks with 225 g sugar to make a frothy mixture. Add the maize flour, dissolved in a little cold milk, and mix well, removing all lumps.

Skim the milk and add to the egg yolk mixture little by little, whisking all the time until it begins to make a light custard (do not allow to cook, as the eggs will set).

Pour into earthenware bowls and leave to cool for a few hours in the refrigerator. Sprinkle with the rest of the sugar and caramelise with a round branding iron.

Flores de Sartén

This dessert, deeply-rooted in Castilian tradition, is mentioned in several literary works, including Don Quijote. Though these "pan flowers" may appear difficult to make, with the right mould they are very easy to prepare, and are absolutely delicious.

Ingredients for 6 people

3 eggs
175 g flour
3/4 cups milk
3 spoonfuls of sugar
1 spoonful of powdered cinnamon
olive oil for frying

Source of the River Mundo (Albacete)

Whisk the eggs in a bowl. Add the milk and, gradually, the flour, to make a thick cream.

Heat plenty of oil in a deep pan, place mould in oil and, when very hot, put it in the bowl with the batter, making sure that it is not completely covered, and place quickly in frying pan. The batter will separate from the mould as it fries. Lightly fry on either side, repeating until all the batter is used up.

Finally, mix sugar with cinnamon and sprinkle on the "flowers".

These are special metal moulds for making "flowers". They are sold at ironmongers', markets and specialised shops in Spain.

Arroz con Leche
(Rice Pudding)

This splendid dessert, found in the cuisine of many Latin countries, costs next to nothing to make and, if prepared carefully, is absolutely delicious.

Ingredients for 6 people

125 g rice
175 g sugar
1 litre of milk
1 sprig of cinnamon
the peel from 1 lemon
powdered cinnamon

Picos de Europa mountains

Heat the milk with the cinnamon and the lemon peel. When it starts to boil, add the rice, previously washed, and simmer for about 20 minutes, stirring with a wooden spoon. Add the sugar and cook for another 10 minutes, stirring all the while to make sure it does not stick.

Once practically all the liquid has been absorbed and a creamy mixture has formed, remove the cinnamon and the lemon peel and pour into bowls; sprinkle with cinnamon and serve cold.